The Bake Sale

by Olive Porter
illustrated by Sarah Beise

HOUGHTON MIFFLIN HARCOURT
School Publishers

Printed in India

ISBN-13: 978-0-547-02304-5
ISBN-10: 0-547-02304-9

2 3 4 5 6 7 8 0940 18 17 16 15 14 13 12 11 10

Ms. Hawkins wanted to take her class on a field trip to a museum. But there was not enough money in the school budget for field trips. Ms. Hawkins knew the class would have to raise money for the field trip. They could start a field trip fund.

Ms. Hawkins discussed the plan with the class. "Does anyone have ideas for raising money?" asked Ms. Hawkins.

Hector said, "We could have a car wash."

Janice said, "We could have a students-against-teachers softball game and sell tickets."

Ms. Hawkins thanked Hector and Janice for their ideas. "It is winter, and winter is not the right time for a car wash or a softball game," she explained. Then she repeated her question. "Does anyone have other ideas for raising money?"

Tina raised her hand. "We could have a bake sale to raise money," she suggested.

"That sounds like a plan that can work," said Ms. Hawkins. The class agreed. They made a list of what each student would bake. "We'll run a test," said Ms. Hawkins. "Please plan to bring in a sample of your baking. We can try the food before the bake sale next week."

The students came in with boxes and bags.
They set the food out on a table. Everyone tried it.
"These muffins are burned," said Celine.

"I guess I left them in the oven too long,"
Tina said.

"This cookie has no taste," said Richard.

"I think I forgot to put in the sugar," Lin said.

"This cupcake is too soggy," said Janice.

"Maybe I mixed the batter too long," Dustin said.

Everyone was disappointed. Hector was staring at the food. He said, "We won't make any money if our food tastes like this."

Ms. Hawkins had a solution. "A friend of mine is a baker. I will ask her to give us a baking lesson. Then we'll be ready for our bake sale."

Ms. Wells was the baker. She came to the school and showed the students how to bake. She showed them how to measure and mix. She showed them how to fill pans and set timers. At the end of the lesson, everyone thanked Ms. Wells.

"Good luck with your bake sale!" said Ms. Wells.

On the day of the bake sale, the students came to school with their food. Ms. Hawkins and the students spread out the food on a big table. There were muffins, cookies, and cakes. There were pies, doughnuts, and brownies. "Everything looks delicious," said Ms. Hawkins.

"I hope everyone else thinks so, too," Janice said.

Students and teachers came to the bake sale, all day long. Ms. Hawkins put all the money that they received in a box. "How much money do we have so far?" Richard asked.

Ms. Hawkins chuckled. "I don't know yet, but this box is getting full."

The bake sale was over when everything had been sold and the table was empty. Ms. Hawkins and her students went back to the classroom.

Ms. Hawkins passed around a plate of cookies. She winked as she said, "Have a cookie while I look in the box and see what we have in our account."

After Ms. Hawkins counted the money, she gave a big smile. She said, "Thank you for your wonderful baking. This was the school's best bake sale. It's the most money any classroom has raised." The students felt happy and proud.

"Now we have enough money to take our field trip to the museum," said Ms. Hawkins

The students cheered. Lin raised her hand. "I have an idea. Let's invite Ms. Wells on our field trip," she suggested.

"That's a good idea, Lin. Without Ms. Wells, we wouldn't be going to the museum!" said Ms. Hawkins.

Responding

✓ TARGET SKILL **Story Structure** Think about where the story took place, who was in it, and what happened. Copy the chart and add details from the story.

Characters Ms. Hawkins	Setting a school
Story Details ?	

Write About It

Text to Self Imagine that your class needs to raise money for a field trip. Use a few sentences to write a fictional narrative about how you and your class would raise money and what trip you'd like to go on.

✔ **TARGET SKILL** **Story Structure** Tell the setting, character, and plot in a story.

✔ **TARGET STRATEGY** **Infer/Predict** Use clues to figure out more about story parts.

GENRE **Realistic fiction** is a story that could happen in real life.